Preparing for Growth at University and College

A Workbook for New Students

Adam Morgan

Sydney, Australia

Copyright © 2025 Adam Morgan

All rights reserved. Except to the extent permitted by law, no part of this publication may be reproduced, distributed, or transmitted in any form or by any means, including photocopying, recording, or other electronic or mechanical methods, without the prior written permission of the author. The author can be contacted via adam-morgan.com.au.

The information contained in this workbook is for educational purposes. No warranties of any kind are declared or implied. By engaging with this workbook, the user agrees that under no circumstances is the author responsible for any damages or losses, direct or indirect, that are incurred as a result of the use of the information contained within this workbook, including, but not limited to, errors, omissions, or inaccuracies.

ISBN 978-0-6456794-5-8

Published by Adam Morgan

Design and Layout:
Ilka Staudinger-Morgan

Contents

Introduction		1
Part A	**Considering Growth**	**3**
	1. Knowledge and Learning	4
	2. Higher-Order Thinking	6
	3. Written Communication	8
	4. Verbal Communication	10
	5. Teamwork	12
	6. Self-Management	14
	7. Problem-Solving	16
	8. Global Citizenship	18
	9. A Growth Area of Your Choice	20
Part B	**Reconsidering Growth**	**23**
	10. Your Strongest Areas	24
	11. Some Improvement Areas	25
	12. Your Support Network	26
	13. A Year from Now	27
Conclusion		29
References		30

Introduction

As a new university/college student, you will embark on an important growth journey. Your institution wants to see you grow in many areas over the next few years and has created a rich environment to help this happen. Throughout these pages, you will start preparing for some of this growth. You will consider a core set of growth opportunities on offer to you and actively engage with them.

After completing this workbook, you will better understand your upcoming growth journey. You will have looked at some of the growth opportunities available to you. You will have considered your current ability levels and identified those areas where further growth is possible. You will also consider how you have grown in the past and how you might grow in the coming years.

Completing this workbook is straightforward. First, you will consider your growth in several important areas. Later, you will reconsider your answers to prepare even more.

This workbook requires you to write entries. In terms of the amount you write and the quality of your entries, this depends on how you have come about engaging with this workbook. If you are completing this workbook as part of your growth preparation, with no institutional expectations or requirements, then the amount you write and the quality of your entries is your decision to make. You can write as little or as much as you like in the spaces provided, and the quality of your entries is also up to you. If completing this workbook is required at your institution, however, it is essential that you clarify what is expected of you. There might be specific expectations regarding the amount you have to write and the quality of your entries.

Part A

Considering Growth

The first part of this workbook presents several growth areas. Your task is to answer the questions related to each growth area. There are nine areas covered in this first part. These are:

- Knowledge and Learning
- Higher-Order Thinking
- Written Communication
- Verbal Communication
- Teamwork
- Self-Management
- Problem-Solving
- Global Citizenship
- A Growth Area of Your Choice

1. Knowledge and Learning

Universities and colleges are places where passionate experts create and disseminate knowledge. Your teachers and support staff have curated the knowledge you will engage with. They have carefully considered what you should be learning and have designed innovative ways to help you acquire this knowledge. Your teachers and support staff will build on the foundations laid by all of those who have helped you to learn in the past (e.g., your past teachers, your family, your friends), and don't forget all the knowledge you have acquired as a self-directed learner. You have acquired a great deal of knowledge up to this point in your life, and you have the potential to learn a lot more over the next few years. You have the potential to become far more knowledgeable than you currently are. However, this depends on what you already know and your motivation to learn more. Please complete the next page to help you prepare for this area of your growth journey.

I am already knowledgeable in the areas I will study at my institution.

○ Strongly disagree ○ Disagree ○ Neither agree nor disagree ○ Strongly agree ○ Agree

I can learn a lot during my studies.

○ Strongly disagree ○ Disagree ○ Neither agree nor disagree ○ Strongly agree ○ Agree

In which areas can you learn a lot?

[   ]

What might prevent you from learning as part of your studies, and how could you overcome any potential barriers?

[   ]

2. Higher-Order Thinking

Universities and colleges are higher education institutions. You will be exposed to complex theories, concepts, and ideas. You will be required to make sense of them, critically evaluate them, apply them in new ways, consider their limitations, and extend their utility, to name a few. You will also be required to critique yourself (e.g., via reflective tasks) and make judgments on your work and that produced by other students (e.g., via self and peer assessment tasks). You might even be required to defend your ideas and opinions (e.g., via debates and presentations to panel members). All these actions involve complex, higher-order thinking. This is a growth opportunity for you. You have the potential to grow in relation to higher-order thinking over the next few years. However, this depends on your current ability levels and your motivation to improve them. Please complete the next page to help you prepare for this area of your growth journey.

I am already good at thinking in the higher-order ways mentioned.

○ Strongly disagree   ○ Disagree   ○ Neither agree nor disagree   ○ Strongly agree   ○ Agree

My higher-order thinking abilities can improve.

○ Strongly disagree   ○ Disagree   ○ Neither agree nor disagree   ○ Strongly agree   ○ Agree

Which aspects of higher-order thinking could you improve?

What might prevent you from improving in relation to higher-order thinking, and how could you overcome any potential barriers?

3. Written Communication

Communicating in the written form will be a central part of your studies. Essays, reports, sections in group reports, short and long answer responses in exams, blog posts, news articles, and presentation slides are some of the ways you might be required to write during your studies. Your writing will often be assessed, with feedback given to help you improve. You might also receive feedback from family members, friends, peers, professionals in support roles, and online tools. Your institution might also have specific initiatives to help you develop in this area (e.g., workshops, courses, drop-in sessions). All this support has the potential to help you grow as a writer. However, this depends on your current ability levels and your motivation to improve them. Please complete the next page to help you prepare for this area of your growth journey.

I am already a good writer.

○ Strongly disagree   ○ Disagree   ○ Neither agree nor disagree   ○ Strongly agree   ○ Agree

My written communication skills can improve.

○ Strongly disagree   ○ Disagree   ○ Neither agree nor disagree   ○ Strongly agree   ○ Agree

Which aspects of your written communication could you improve?

What might prevent you from improving as a writer, and how could you overcome any potential barriers?

4. Verbal Communication

Your student experiences will also involve communicating verbally. You will participate in many verbal-based activities during your studies, such as class discussions, debates, role-plays, and group work. You might also have to make class presentations or similar performances (e.g., demonstrations, pitches). There will also be a lot of informal verbal communication during your studies, such as speaking with other students, staff members, and people in the broader community. Your institution might also have specific initiatives to help you develop in this area (e.g., workshops, courses, sessions). You have the potential to grow as a verbal communicator during your studies. However, this depends on your current ability levels and your motivation to improve them. Please complete the next page to help you prepare for this area of your growth journey.

I am already a good verbal communicator.

○ Strongly disagree   ○ Disagree   ○ Neither agree nor disagree   ○ Strongly agree   ○ Agree

My verbal communication skills can improve.

○ Strongly disagree   ○ Disagree   ○ Neither agree nor disagree   ○ Strongly agree   ○ Agree

Which aspects of verbal communication could you improve?

What might prevent you from improving as a verbal communicator, and how could you overcome any potential barriers?

5. Teamwork

Your educational institution will give you the opportunity to work with others in groups many times throughout your studies. You will participate in group assignments/projects and class discussion groups. You might also be part of a study group, a sports team, a social club, or a student committee. You will also make new friends during your studies, and do things together with them in groups. You have the potential to become a much better team player over the next few years. Here are just some of the many teamwork abilities you have the potential to develop:*

- Listening actively
- Communicating constructively
- Helping
- Leading
- Following the lead of others
- Treating others with respect
- Responding to conflict
- Motivating others
- Contributing to group meetings
- Working as a problem-solver
- Showing flexibility
- Demonstrating reliability
- Fostering constructive group climates

However, this depends on your current ability levels and your motivation to improve them. Please complete the next page to help you prepare for this area of your growth journey.

---

* Drawn from frameworks proposed by Brounstein (2002), Wheelan (2015), and the Association of American Colleges and Universities (AAC&U).

I am already a good team player.

○ Strongly disagree   ○ Disagree   ○ Neither agree nor disagree   ○ Strongly agree   ○ Agree

I can improve as a team player.

○ Strongly disagree   ○ Disagree   ○ Neither agree nor disagree   ○ Strongly agree   ○ Agree

Which teamwork abilities could you improve?

What might prevent you from improving as a team player, and how could you overcome any potential barriers?

6. Self-Management

There are many demands placed on university and college students. There is never enough time to do everything you need to do. There are classes to attend, class preparation to do, research to be undertaken, papers to write, online tasks to engage with, and group meetings to attend, to name a few. You must do all this along with the numerous other demands on your time, such as work commitments, family responsibilities, co-curricular/extracurricular activities, appointments, maintaining friendships, and making time for yourself. How you go about managing these competing demands will be your responsibility. You will be expected to self-manage. Again, this is a growth opportunity for you. You have the potential to grow in the area of self-management over the next few years. However, this depends on your current ability levels and your motivation to improve them. Please complete the next page to help you prepare for this area of your growth journey.

I am already good at self-management.

○ Strongly disagree ○ Disagree ○ Neither agree nor disagree ○ Strongly agree ○ Agree

I can improve in the area of self-management.

○ Strongly disagree ○ Disagree ○ Neither agree nor disagree ○ Strongly agree ○ Agree

Which aspects of self-management could you improve?

What might prevent you from improving in the area of self-management, and how could you overcome any potential barriers?

7. Problem-Solving

Universities and colleges are complex places that work with complicated issues. Dealing with ill-defined and challenging problems is the norm. The teachers and support staff at your institution constantly operate with complexity. They research and teach complex topics. In higher education, they also expect their students to operate in this complex space. The topics you will be exposed to are very complex. The assignments you will undertake are complex and challenging. The dynamics within your group assignments/projects will sometimes be challenging. The management of your workload will also be challenging at times. You will constantly be solving problems. This is another opportunity for you to grow, this time as a problem-solver. However, this depends on your current ability levels and your motivation to improve them. Please complete the next page to help you prepare for this area of your growth journey.

I am already good at problem-solving.

○ Strongly disagree   ○ Disagree   ○ Neither agree nor disagree   ○ Strongly agree   ○ Agree

I can improve as a problem-solver.

○ Strongly disagree   ○ Disagree   ○ Neither agree nor disagree   ○ Strongly agree   ○ Agree

Which aspects of problem-solving could you improve?

What might prevent you from improving as a problem-solver, and how could you overcome any potential barriers?

8. Global Citizenship

Universities and colleges have considerable diversity within them. The teaching and support staff at your institution are diverse. They come from different parts of the world or country. They have different upbringings, experiences, and world views. The students at your institution are equally diverse. You will be fortunate to experience this diversity at a much closer level. You will listen to them in class. You will work alongside them during in-class activities. You will work with them on group assignments/projects. They will help and support you. You will learn from them. You will gain insights into how they think, solve problems, and communicate, to name a few. The topics you will engage with will also be diverse. You will be introduced to a vast array of theories and concepts. You have the potential to be shaped by all this diversity. Your views have the potential to be enriched. You have the potential to become more knowledgeable about local, national, and international affairs. You have the potential to understand the modern world better and how one operates in diverse environments. You have the potential to grow as a global citizen. However, this depends on your current levels and your motivation to improve them. Please complete the next page to help you prepare for this area of your growth journey.

I am already an experienced global citizen.

○ Strongly disagree   ○ Disagree   ○ Neither agree nor disagree   ○ Strongly agree   ○ Agree

I can improve as a global citizen.

○ Strongly disagree   ○ Disagree   ○ Neither agree nor disagree   ○ Strongly agree   ○ Agree

Which aspects of global citizenship could you improve?

What might prevent you from improving as a global citizen, and how could you overcome any potential barriers?

9. A Growth Area of Your Choice

Up to this point, we have covered some of the main growth areas at university and college. There are, however, many others, such as:

- Creativity
- Ethics
- Leadership
- Lifelong Learning
- Using Technology
- Entrepreneurship
- Quantitative Literacy
- Inquiry and Analysis
- Information Literacy
- Visual Communication

This is your chance to write about an additional growth area you would like to develop during your studies. It can be one that is listed above or one not listed. It might be one specific to your institution's mission or one that you feel the need to develop. It might be an area where you are already skilled and want to improve. Alternatively, it is an area where you lack skill and want to develop it from scratch. Please complete below and the next page to help you prepare for this area of your growth journey.

What is your selected growth area?

I am already good in my selected growth area.

○ Strongly disagree　　○ Disagree　　○ Neither agree nor disagree　　○ Strongly agree　　○ Agree

I can improve in my selected growth area.

○ Strongly disagree　　○ Disagree　　○ Neither agree nor disagree　　○ Strongly agree　　○ Agree

Which aspects of your selected growth area could you improve?

[   ]

What might prevent you from improving in your selected growth area, and how could you overcome any potential barriers?

[   ]

Part B

Reconsidering Growth

In Part A of this workbook, you answered questions related to your potential growth. In this second part, you will now reconsider your answers. This reconsidering is very important to do. It will help you see the bigger picture of your growth journey ahead. Before we begin Part B, it is important that you look again at your answers in Part A. Once you have done this, there are four more short tasks. These relate to:

- Your Strongest Areas
- Some Improvement Areas
- Your Support Network
- A Year from Now

10. Your Strongest Areas

In the previous part of this workbook (Part A), you rated your current ability levels in various growth areas. Some of these areas were most likely rated higher than others.

Which three areas did you rate the highest?

1. _____

2. _____

3. _____

How have you become skilled in these areas?

11. Some Improvement Areas

In the previous part of this workbook (Part A), you also rated how much you could improve in each growth area.

Which three areas do you believe are most in need of improvement?

1. _____

2. _____

3. _____

How are you going to improve in these areas?

12. Your Support Network

As a new student, you will embark on a growth journey. It is unrealistic to expect this journey always to be easy. This is why your institution has many support structures to help you. There are many people and services in place to support you.

In the space below, list some of the support people/services available (who) and how they will be able to help you grow (how).

Who?   **How?**

_____   _____

_____   _____

_____   _____

_____   _____

_____   _____

_____   _____

13. A Year from Now

Consider this scenario: It is a year from now. You have been at your institution for an entire year. Everything is going well. You are enjoying being a student at your institution. You have applied yourself and have been successful. You have taken advantage of the support available to you and have grown considerably.

In the text box below, write about your growth in the last year. In which areas have you grown the most? How did this growth come about? What does this growth mean to you?

Conclusion

This workbook has allowed you to prepare for the upcoming growth journey at your institution. You have the potential to grow in many areas over the next few years. You have just looked at this potential growth and written about it. Hopefully, you can see how much potential growth there is in front of you.

As you put your completed workbook in a safe place, take a moment to think about what you have done. You have considered an essential part of being a student at a university/college—growing. By doing so, you have shown a commitment to growing and reaching your full potential. It is now time to demonstrate this commitment and see what happens.

References

Association of American Colleges and Universities (AAC&U). *VALUE Rubrics - Teamwork*. Retrieved from https://www.aacu.org/initiatives/value-initiative/value-rubrics/value-rubrics-teamwork

Brounstein, M. (2002). *Managing teams for dummies*. New York: Wiley.

Wheelan, S. A. (2015). *Creating effective teams: A guide for members and leaders* (5th Ed.). Thousand Oaks, CA: Sage.

www.ingramcontent.com/pod-product-compliance
Lightning Source LLC
Chambersburg PA
CBHW051159290426
44109CB00022B/2511